Scholastic
CLIFFORD
THE BIG RED DOG

Phon **Reading P**

A Little Book About Red

by Francie Alexander
Illustrated by Steve Haefele

Based on the books by Norman Bridwell

SCHOLASTIC INC.
New York   Toronto   London   Auckland   Sydney
Mexico City   New Delhi   Hong Kong   Buenos Aires

Time to get up!

Clifford barks at
the window for
Emily Elizabeth to get up.

She giggles and hops
out of bed.
It is cold so she puts on
fuzzy red slippers.

Emily Elizabeth likes red.

The kettle makes a loud whistle.

Emily Elizabeth runs to the table.
She has a little red hat on her head.
She has big red boots on her feet.

Emily Elizabeth likes red.

Emily Elizabeth and Clifford go to school. Clifford keeps her out of the puddles.
She snuggles and pats his head.
"Thank you for keeping my red boots clean."
Emily Elizabeth likes red.

Today Emily Elizabeth's class visits the fire station.
It is so cold that the kids wiggle into their jackets.

"Welcome!" says Fire Chief Campbell.

Miss Carrington blows her whistle. "Stay in line," she tells the class.

"Look at the bright red fire truck,"
Miss Carrington says.

Fire Chief Campbell lets them climb on the truck.

What fun!

Emily Elizabeth likes red.

Back at school, the kids
settle down.
They read books and
do riddles.
They get red paper
and crayons.

Emily Elizabeth likes red.

Today is Valentine's Day.
Emily Elizabeth makes
four little valentines
and one big one.
She writes in the middle
of the big heart:

"Roses are red,
You are, too.
I like red..."

"...but **I** **love** you!"